THE ULTRA-SHORT

THE FOURTEENTH ANNUAL
ULTRA-SHORT COMPETITION

THE PRIMAVERA PRESS
FOR THE
UNIVERSITY OF MAINE AT MACHIAS
2017 - 18

Cover Image: Marcus Stone (1840-1921). *Her First Love Letter*. (1888). Auckland Art Gallery. Public domain.

Print ISSN: 2160-634X
Online ISSN: 2160-6331

ISBN-13: 978-1-7329991-0-7

TABLE OF CONTENTS

THE ULTRA-SHORT

THE FOURTEENTH ANNUAL
ULTRA-SHORT COMPETITION

THE PRIMAVERA PRESS
FOR THE
UNIVERSITY OF MAINE AT MACHIAS
2017 - 18

A Day in the Life
Debra Kirouac
Prize for Humor

Nora shoved her house key into the lock after a long day of pretending to be busy at work – a soul-crushing place where dreams went to die – but somebody had to bring home the store-brand bacon. And that "somebody" was Nora.

Her young son was behind her and, in his excitement to greet their meowing cat, caught the toe of his stiff Star Wars boot on the heel of Mom's black suede pump, sending her flying, coincidentally, into their shoe rack.

Cheap footwear flew through the air, landing around Nora like a chalk outline of a dead body. The panicked cat bolted across Nora's backside, puncturing her left buttock and shredding the other one like grated cheese. Her son squealed with misplaced delight, chasing the feline down the stairs. The pain of Nora's wounds was exquisite, like the bottle of merlot that was just out of her reach.

Nominated for a Pushcart Prize in 2017

DEBRA KIROUAC
A DAY IN THE LIFE

Debra Kirouac is a Mainer at heart, but now calls Connecticut "home." She is very happy to be included in this fine edition, and looks forward to reading it cover to cover.

TROMPE L'OEIL
CLARE MARSH
PRIZE FOR POETRY

Wheeled into the dark room,
rhythmic pain pulses
through me on the couch.

A squirt of cold jelly,
the press of the handset
skating over expectant skin.

Relief at the image — the spinal curl,
thumb in mouth, fist raised in greeting.
A surviving twin?

Sorry. The sonographer
refreshes the screen.
The last patient's ghost baby left in error

vanishes to reveal

a void.

NOMINATED FOR A PUSHCART PRIZE IN 2017

CLARE MARSH
TROMPE L'OEIL

As an adoption social worker Clare writes reports based on extraordinary life stories – from children abandoned in overseas orphanages to multiple murderers. She lives in the Weald of Kent, known as the Garden of England, where she has recently completed her MA in Creative Writing at the University of Kent, Canterbury.

SUMMER LOVE
CHRISTY STOFKO
PRIZE FOR PROSE

Each June we moved our twin beds onto the sleeping porch on the second floor of the brick duplex my mother and I shared with 85-year-old widowed Mrs. Howard who lived below us on the first floor. My mother would wash and dry the bed sheets, using a water-filled glass soda bottle capped by a yellow plastic sprinkler topper to remoisten the wrinkled sheets before ironing them. The mixture of the spray starch scent combined with the feel of the stiff, smooth cotton sheets against my five-year-old legs never failed to thrill yet reassure me each time I climbed into bed.

The unheated, unused-for-nine-months room was our summer clubhouse. The glow of the reading lamp perched on the makeshift nightstand between our beds illuminated the nights. My love for my mother was unwavering and absolute. I thought it would go on forever.

NOMINATED FOR A PUSHCART PRIZE IN 2017

CHRISTY STOFKO
SUMMER LOVE

Just as Clark Kent had an alter ego—Christy Stofko also has a split identity. She is a runner and a hiker in the Arizona desert by day and a wordsmith and dreamer by night.

ALMOST VALHALLA
GEORGE NEWCASTLE
PRIZE FOR SLICE OF LIFE

Harold Loughman, visiting lecturer in Norse Studies, tried to ignore Theda Johanssen's bratwurst-like fingers, worm-odored boots, and fingernails-on-chalkboard voice. But when she uh-ehm-ed for the forty-sixth time in fifty-four minutes, he tapped on her office door and asked, "Could you use a piece of hard candy?"

"I don't need anything from you, Viking man," she replied.

The next morning three colleagues met him outside his office door. One said, "How dare you add a comma to our 'Modernists Unite' poster!" Before he could form the words "direct address," Two stuffed a red rag in his mouth, and Three tied his hands behind his back.

Harnessed into a raft at the edge of the Beatrice M. Hella Pond behind the library, he watched One light the floating pyre.

With eyes fixed on the distant blue mountains tickled by the long fingers of cirrostratus clouds, Harold believed he was almost in Valhalla.

NOMINATED FOR A PUSHCART PRIZE IN 2017

GEORGE NEWCASTLE
ALMOST VALHALLA

George Newcastle began his public writing career with the submission of "Almost Valhalla." An engineer by training, he has always found time for rock climbing, community theater, contra dancing, and needlepoint. He lives with his wife and three daughters in Valhalla.

THE JANITOR'S BROOM
DANNY P. BARBARE

As if sweeping time
  away
straw for straw
  by and by
its handle is quicker
  than the hour
  hand
good as wood— tock.

DANNY P. BARBARE
THE JANITOR'S BROOM

Danny P. Barbare has recently been published in *Along the Shore*, *Halcyon Days*, *Fredericksburg Literary & Art Review*, and *Birmingham Arts Journal*. He works at and has attended Greenville Technical College. His poetry has been nominated for Best of the Net by *Assisi Online Journal*, and his poetry has won the Jim Gitting's Award.

POST-EUHEMERISM
MICHELE BARON

The rising sun illuminated the blank space around me. I stretched, alone, eager to begin.

With my hands I mixed together the magic that would become stars, and with all my strength flung them to the emptiness above. I gathered earth, and precious things, for plants and living creatures of all kinds.

I cleaned up the traces of my work, visiting every plant and creature, making sure all was balanced, nothing left out. Daylight waned. I smelled the wafting aroma of the fruits of the day; sounds of bustling preparations for nightfall surrounded me.

I had forgotten water! I caused it to flow, and surveyed the vastness of my creation.

...

"Is that *paint* all over your ceiling and clothes?" my mother shrieked from the doorway. "Dinner's ready! Finish your bath and come downstairs!"

I smiled. The ceiling's glow-paint stars would shine brightly when the lights were turned off for sleep.

MICHELE BARON
POST-EUHEMERISM

World traveler, Fulbright Scholar, author, visual/performance artist Michele Baron just relocated after living three years in Kyrgyzstan, and marvels as life continues to demonstrate that even the most chaotic of days can seem normal. Recipient of a Citation for Contributions to the Arts from Maryland General Assembly Senator Susan C. Lee, Ms. Baron has self-published three novelettes to date: *A Modest Menu: Poverty, Hunger and Food Security, in Poetry and Prose*; *A Holiday Carol: A Modern Interpretation of Dickens' "A Christmas Carol"*; and *blue wings unfolding.*

BOUND
SALLY BASMAJIAN

I want to throw myself at Grandmother's tiny feet and beg for mercy but I can't. My mother and her friends restrain me.

"Be brave." My mother's eyes are worried. I mustn't disgrace her.

As Grandmother tightens my bandages, I feel a bone snap and smother a shriek. Behind closed eyelids, I see pinwheels of color in shades of agonized red.

I know when this is over, I'll never walk freely again. I'll be in constant pain.

But I'll be desirable.

"Continue." I say the word through clenched teeth.

Grandmother gives me an approving nod.

"You'll do, girl."

I know she's right. I'll survive this. Others in my family have, and gone on to make brilliant marriages.

I hear my bones crunch, like the wing of a sparrow in the beak of an owl, but I am motionless. Through mists of burgundy I imagine my bridegroom's face.

It radiates love.

SALLY BASMAJIAN
BOUND

Sally Basmajian is an executive escapee from the broadcasting industry. She's a short fiction and memoir dabbler, and struggles ever forward on a novel. Recently, her stories have appeared in *The Globe and Mail*, *Calliope*, and more. She lives in Niagara-on-the-Lake, Canada with her demanding sheltie and her understanding husband.

THE GEESE
MARA BUCK

"Gonna be leaving your Mom. You stay strong." The man ruffled his son's hair.

"How come?"

"Shit happens, boy. Shit happens."

"Can we still go hunting and fishing?"

"Why not? We'll fire off a couple right now. Get some geese."

"Dad, isn't the season next month?"

"Don't matter none. Who's gonna know? Damn rules."

They reach the marsh and the air vibrates with the voices of the birds.

"Are they talking?" the boy asks.

"Gibberish, like your ma. Ain't no sense to it."

The geese take wing and the man raises his gun. He's a good shot and drops two in succession. The boy rushes over to the fallen birds. The dying geese struggle closer together, their wings overlapping. They've been banded, but the bands are plain gold, inscriptions worn thin by loyalty.

"Well, ain't that peculiar." The man scowls.

"Daddy, didn't you know? Geese mate for life."

MARA BUCK
THE GEESE

Mara Buck writes in a self-constructed hideaway in the Maine woods. Awarded/short-listed by *Faulkner-Wisdom*, *Hackney*, *Carpe Articulum*, *Balticon*. Recent firsts include F. Scott Fitzgerald Poetry Prize, The Binnacle Prize. Published in *Hektoen International*, *Drunken Boat*, *HuffPost*, *Crack the Spine*, *Blue Fifth*, *Pithead Chapel*, *Tishman*, *Whirlwind*, plus in numerous print anthologies. She has just been awarded First Prize in the Scottish Arts Club International Short Story Contest.

MEMORY
TOWER OF LONDON, WWI CENTENNIAL, 2014
SARAH CARLETON

Acres of ceramic poppies surround the castle.
I heard they took weeks to plant.

They're brilliant for a moment brief as life,
spilling over the wall, flooding the moat,

a river of red for color-thirsty visitors.
In our black travel clothes, we press together

and gaze down at a flow of crimson so audacious
it bleeds through our tendency to forget.

A few days later, we wedge our way in again
to watch volunteers pick the poppies

and lay them back in their boxes.
They labor with backs bent

like Millet's peasant women.
The poppies ebb; the muddy swath widens.

SARAH CARLETON
MEMORY
TOWER OF LONDON, WWI CENTENNIAL, 2014

Sarah Carleton writes poetry, edits fiction, plays the banjo and raises her son in Tampa, Florida. Her poems have appeared in numerous publications, including *Houseboat, Off the Coast, Shark Reef, Wild Violet, The Binnacle, Cider Press Review, Nimrod, Ekphrastic, Chattahoochee Review, Kindred, Spillway, Tar River Poetry* and *Crab Orchard Review*.

THE IOWA RIVER AS MY SELF-DIAGNOSED MARFAN SYNDROME
MICHELLE CHEN

Along the water there are burls of smoke
from catfish boats, cicada-sized.

Clapboard toolshed's blurry
behind a patch of coneflowers,

hovel paint and flaked petals as a sandhill
crane wrings a frog apart on the riverbed,

its body mirroring the odd curve of my mouth, chest, spine.
That afternoon I walked into mud

and my chest closed in. *I'm a shelf*, I said.
A hare struck open, comically long.

The Mississippi swallowed your father
when he saw his daughter with an aluminum boy.

We went home pretty well,
pretty fast. My knuckles brushed

a little hill, crumple rug,
red ants spilling like grease.

MICHELLE CHEN
THE IOWA RIVER AS MY SELF-DIAGNOSED MARFAN
SYNDROME

Michelle Chen is a writer who takes inspiration from her home, New York City, as well as from her travels. She was born in Singapore and spent her early years in China before immigrating to the United States at the age of four. Her work has appeared in *Prairie Schooner*, *Rattle*, *Bat City Review*, and elsewhere. She has attended various writing workshops including the Iowa Young Writers' Studio with the support of the National Society of Arts and Letters, and she is currently a sophomore at the University of Massachusetts Amherst.

THE DAIRY QUEEN
SALLY CLARK

Heading west into the night,
we moseyed into Sonora, TX,
just in time for late night shakes
and nachos at the all-night Dairy Queen.
In the stainless bathroom stall next to mine,
I hear her unmistakable heaves and wonder
should we cancel our order? Too late, I fear,
until I see her return to the dining room,
all pale-face skin and protruding bones of her,
smiling, victorious,
she and her boyfriend speaking French,
a trembling stalk of relief that
even in this soft-serve arcade of cellulite blizzards
and bulging burgers, she had dodged
the bullet of her salvation, so close,
she could almost taste it.

SALLY CLARK
THE DAIRY QUEEN

Sally Clark lives and writes in Fredericksburg, TX. Her poetry has been widely published and won numerous awards across the country. Sally's poems have won honorable mention in *The Binnacle* Ultra-Short Competition in 2012 and 2016. You can follow her at www.sallyclark.info and read her poetry at http://ifollowfredericksburg.com

"FOR GOOD"
KATHLEEN CLAUSON

From my upstairs window, I look down at the moonflowers. Their glowing full-moon faces make me think of Mother's garden, moonflowers tucked into every unflowered space.

I stayed with my parents for several weeks following Dad's surgery. I looked forward to a hot lavender bath and grabbed a plush rainbow-striped bath towel. When she saw it, she scolded me. "I was saving those towels for good. Next time, just ask."

Dish towels were no exception. When they remodeled the hall linen closet I removed a treasure trove of dish towels that filled three large laundry baskets. None were for everyday; maybe three dozen were Christmas towels, the rest were "for good."

In the dark, my garden looks well-groomed; in daylight it is a jungle. My husband discovered my entire collection of tea towels are "for good." I also have an off-limits stash of dish towels. Only the moonflowers know why.

KATHLEEN CLAUSON
"FOR GOOD"

Kathleen Clauson lives in a tiny town, four hours from Chicago, where there are more cats than people. She is the author of numerous published works and boasts that her greatest work has appeared in the *Binnacle*'s Ultra-Short editions. She continues to be inspired by home-towns and everyday life.

GRAND THEFT
CHARLIE COLEMAN

"Maggie, you look exasperated," said Steve, the bartender. "You've got that I'm not getting any decent tips look".

"The cook is so slow he's stealing my tips," Maggie retorted.

"That's a shame."

"Well, it's almost to be expected," said Maggie. "He's already stolen my heart."

CHARLIE COLEMAN
GRAND THEFT

Charlie Coleman is a writer living in Brooklyn, New York. His work has appeared in previous Ultra Short Competitions, *Pulp Metal Magazine* and *The Subway Chronicles*.

GENTLEMEN'S AGREEMENT
ROBERT M. CRAIG

The Lieutenant checked his regiment. All in their places, with the new weapons center front. At the distant trumpet call, he looked downfield to the assembling enemy. They started toward him, stately trotting, banners waving, then the gallop.

He paused, looking at this forward charge in horror and shuddering. Spurring his horse onward, he shouted to his Sergeant, "hold fire. I'm surrendering." With white scarf waving, he yanked his mount to a halt, begging the enemy officer: "Listen to my terms."

The Lieutenant returned to his troops who, now ordered, lugged tree stumps, boulders, and encampment trash to the field's center. At his command, the new Gatling guns opened fire. The awesome scythe shredded all to unrecognizable objects.

The enemy officer waved the Lieutenant forward and spoke: "Our ghastly fate avoided, we accept your terms most gratefully, and leave this field of honor. And may we never meet again."

ROBERT M. CRAIG
GENTLEMEN'S AGREEMENT

Robert Craig, PhD, is a retired high school science teacher/adjunct Assoc. Instructor for local universities in central Indiana. He is a professional woodwind musician who has performed overseas and currently with local ensembles. He continues writing short and novel length fiction, plus researching paranormal events as a skeptic.

DECISION TIME
BARRY DEARBORN

Septuagenarian brothers Dan and Tom, retired Army reservists, are engaged in ardent conversation.

"Ain't our battle, Dan. Belongs to our kids' generation."

"Protecting freedom is every citizen's duty. Being chipped away by this new administration, Tom. Just getting started."

"Done fought our wars. Gotta follow the Constitution, don't they?"

"You'd hope, but conservatives and liberals interpret it differently. Our sons and daughters have families. Our country needs our military skills."

"Ain't *that* bad. Be back to normal next term. Not gonna risk my golden years."

"We must! Our cherished freedoms are disappearing. We're becoming another Russia. Resistance action must begin now. Our parent's birth state got it right – Live Free or Die. Sooner or later, you'll have to choose sides. I'm joining the Underground Freedom Militia tomorrow. Are you coming?"

Tom spat forcibly, sighed, and then muttered "all frick'n unbelievable." Hugging Dan, he whispered, "Maybe later. Stay safe, dear brother."

BARRY DEARBORN
DECISION TIME

Barry Dearborn's interest in writing sprang from a dream in 2007. He has written twenty short stories, one poem, a sci-fi novella and a suspense novel, *Caught Between Evil and Crazy* (the latter in final edit). He is an active member of the Alaska Writers Guild and their Bi-monthly Writing Contest coordinator.

IN A RESTAURANT
ANTHONY DEGREGORIO

The wife asks another waitress for a spoon after sweet Ginger, smiling Ginger, gives them coffee and leaves the table. A few minutes later, Ginger returns. "Want more coffee, sir?" she asks, even though his cup is 5/6 full.

"Yes, thank you, Ginger. I would!" She pours and leaves, but does not smile.

He says, "I think she urinated in it because you asked someone else for the spoons!"

Later, customers at another table who were seated after them get their food first. "See, I told you!"

"Well, I just wish we could get more coffee without appealing to the pope!" the wife says.

"Have to wait till she has to pee again," he says looking at his watch, wondering if Ginger shaves her armpits.

ANTHONY DeGREGORIO
IN A RESTAURANT

Anthony DeGregorio's poetry has appeared or is forth-coming in *The Westchester Review*, *The Maine Review*, and the Main Street Rag anthology, *Of Burgers & Barrooms*. His essays were also published in the *Eastern Iowa Review* and youandmemagazine.com.

OBSESSION
LIZ DOLAN

Sleek-suited and high-heeled,
she busies herself in the world.
But all she thinks of is his long lashes
feathering his brown eyes
and returning to their nest
which she cushions for him with down.
She lets fall satin from her thighs
and bears the ache of a thing ending.
The first frost has already caught the tomatoes
and the red globes have burst.

LIZ DOLAN
OBSESSION

Liz Dolan's first poetry collection, *They Abide,*was nominated for The Robert McGovern Prize, Ashland University. Her second, *A Secret of Long Life,* nominated for a Pushcart, has been published by Cave Moon Press. A nine-time Pushcart nominee and winner of Best of the Web, she was a finalist for Best of the Net 2014. She won The Nassau Prize for Nonfiction, 2011 and the same prize for fiction, 2015.

GRANDFATHER CLOCK
EUNICE-GRACE M. DOMINGO

Every moment that ever was is documented in his hands
Repeated tandems like rituals elbow past my ears
He remembers no memories, yet he knows each passing
    date
Another day under his belt – he moves on like fate

My grandfather, blood bound, sinks into the hours
                    does he recall the birth of everything
he ticks away, creating silence
    repeating repetitions but not very well

Could I gaze at his glazed eyes forever
            seeing the past, but never knowing
            her

I come home and Grandpa has fallen over,
    his glass is gone on the floor
he spilled all of history on my carpet
    I thought I saw Napoleon in the kitchen
He ticks onward
Like a cavalry pressing against the war

EUNICE-GRACE M. DOMINGO
GRANDFATHER CLOCK

Eunice is a freelance writer from Ireland. Born in Dublin—now based in Belfast—she has also lived in Belgium, Japan, the US, and South Africa. Eunice has worked in educational publishing for over twelve years, and she writes fiction whenever the courage prevails.

DANCE
CHRISTINA WOŚ DONNELLY

This tango, tense and Argentine,
a sometimes vicious samba.

Here a winter fire would be most welcome.

Hellos echo from empty walls.
All the light switches on the wrong side.

CHRISTINA WOŚ DONNELLY
DANCE

Christina Woś Donnelly's poem, "Recessional," won the Prize for Best Cadence in the Tenth Annual Ultra-Short Competition. She is honored to have her work included for the seventh time. More at Poets & Writers Directory: http://www.pw.org/content/christina_wos_donnelly

THE LESSER
JENNIFER L. FREED

Her fingers tremble as she pens the note, then pins it safe inside the pocket of his shirt. Such thin cloth to shield him across the miles. She kisses his nose, says his brave-boy journey begins soon. "And drink," she adds. "Brave boys are always thirsty, so drink." She ruffles his hair, turns to hide her eyes. She has paid a good *coyote*, the one her aunt's neighbor recommended. Still, she's heard of exploitation, molestation, dehydration. She's heard of injured stragglers left beneath the beating sun. And yet, for her last son, she chooses this. This, the lesser risk.

JENNIFER L. FREED
THE LESSER

Jennifer L Freed's poetry has recently appeared or is forthcoming in *Amsterdam Quarterly*, *Worcester Review*, and others. Her chapbook, *These Hands Still Holding*, was a finalist in the 2013 New Women's Voices contest. She writes, teaches, and raises her family in Massachusetts. Website: jfreed.weebly.com.

Recent work appears or is forthcoming in Atlanta Review, Amsterdam Quarterly, Worcester Review, and others.

I KNOW ABOUT PIGS
JOYCE FROHN

After Barny's death, the animals had to go. First the cows and now the last pig, the boar. "I don't need help." The driver said. He drove the boar up the tailgate ramp of the truck, the boar twisted on the ramp and beat him down. He drove it up the ramp and it jumped off the tailgate. He drove it up the ramp and it knocked him down. It was snapping.

She got a bushel basket and lined the pig up so it's rump was facing the truck tailgate and pushed the bushel basket over its head. The pig tried to back out of the bushel basket and she went up the ramp until it had backed itself into the truck. She slammed the tailgate. "You know about pigs. You get him out."

JOYCE FROHN
I KNOW ABOUT PIGS

Joyce Frohn is married with a teen-aged daughter. She has two cats and a lizard. The pet she misses most is her deceased slime mold. She credits her grandma, the hero of this story, with her love of, and understanding of, animals.

EVERYONE DIES ALONE
JOE GIORDANO

Everyone dies alone.

I'll be in Intensive Care. Sad-eyed loved ones will gather. I'll rally to coax a smile, but I'll be a mirror of their future, and they'll be relieved to leave.

I'll long to have my life back, but in the stillness of 3 am, I'll accept my fate. The cycle of pain will return. I'll reach for the nurse's call button, the source of soothing morphine. In the dim white and yellow lights of the vital-sign monitor, a lady in blue will appear. My thumb won't press the button. The lady will beckon; I'll reach for her. Life is precious, until it's not, but I won't die alone.

JOE GIORDANO
EVERYONE DIES ALONE

Joe's stories have appeared in more than ninety magazines including *Bartleby Snopes*, *The Saturday Evening Post*, *decomP*, *The Summerset Review*, and *Shenandoah*. His novel, *Birds of Passage*, *An Italian Immigrant Coming of Age Story*, was published by *Harvard Square Editions* October 2015. His second novel, *Appointment with ISIL, an Anthony Provati Thriller* will be published by HSE in May 2017. Read the first chapters and sign up for his blog at http://joe-giordano.com/.

DYING WOULD BE CHEAPER
MIRANDA DIVETT GONZÁLEZ

Craig held the bill between two fingers as if it were a dead animal, then slit the envelope with a tomato knife and extracted a fat stack of papers folded into thirds. Setting the other sheets aside, he scanned the last page until his eyes rested on the final line: $50,000 for his ruptured appendix! Ah, but he had balked at the $250 per-paycheck premium. An angry pulse beat at his temple. He slammed the statement onto the glass coffee table, which shattered on impact. Jagged shards impaled his fist. Briefly, he entertained the thought of grabbing another piece of glass and slicing his wrists, letting the blood run. Instead, he wound a dish towel around the red mess and asked his wife to drive him to the emergency room.

MIRANDA DIVETT GONZÁLEZ
DYING WOULD BE CHEAPER

Miranda Divett González is an MFA student at the University of Texas at El Paso. Her short fiction and nonfiction have appeared in *Monkeybicycle*, *GNU Journal*, and *Heart Online*. She lives in San Antonio, Texas, where she and her husband are raising three bilingual children.

ANNA'S SONG
TRACY L. GRIMALDI

A soft breeze whispers through the open window kissing my face. I close my eyes and the softness becomes Anna's lips.

Outside, gathered at the base of a feeder, mourning doves bask in the warmth of the fading sun. Their song holds me captive. The mournful melody contains the words I cannot speak—the tears I cannot cry—the sadness I cannot escape. It alights on my sorrow.

The phone's ring places my thoughts on hold.

"Hello?"

"Hi, Dad." My son's voice is hesitant, "how are you doing?"

"Good," I lie. Two years today and I'm still not good.

"I really miss Mom."

"I miss her too."

We say our goodbyes as the sun is ending its day's journey. Night's approach signals the doves to fade away to settle into their nests like the pain that has settled into my soul—familiar and at home.

TRACY L. GRIMALDI
ANNA'S SONG

Tracy Grimaldi has a fondness for the Ultra-Short genre. As an animal rescuer and caregiver she finds stories in observing their lives. Her work has won awards and has been published in various anthologies. She lives in Loveland, Ohio.

TAXING
DEBBIE OKUN HILL

Her head slumped like a number zero
tired and overworked at the kitchen table.
Surrounded by income tax receipts
the aftertaste of bills and more debt
(nothing glamourous about T4s and T5s
nor the line totaling her net worth)
she counts and recounts the hardships:
friends lost to cancer, noisy neighbors
children calculating and estranged.
Her mother once told her
"Be strong. Pay your own way".
The advice once too taxing
like an old-fashioned adding machine
too heavy to carry too long
left her grounded, comforted by her future audits
as a Chartered Accountant.

DEBBIE OKUN HILL
TAXING

Debbie Okun Hill is a Canadian poet, blogger, and author of *Tarnished Trophies* (Black Moss Press, 2014). To date, over 400 of her poems have been published in such publications as *Existere*, *Vallum*, and *The Windsor Review* in Canada plus earlier issues of *The Binnacle* and *LUMMOX* in the United States.

OBITUARY FOR LAZARUS
MICHAEL JEWELL

Who hears his cry beneath the burned-out light
in the alleyway behind the Laundromat
when four teenage boys beat him up
for the thrill of it? He pleads, then yells,
slurring insults as he falls,

struck senseless and freezing overnight.
Who cares for a wino, stinking like Lazarus
when they find him, covered by an inch
of snow? He is survived by a circle
of curious bystanders who watch

as EMS workers lift him into their ambulance:
a seed with a heart of flame extinguished,
a warning lodged in darkness, one of thirty
possible words in the language of crows
roughly translated as "thirst."

MICHAEL JEWELL
OBITUARY FOR LAZARUS

Michael Jewell is a poet, painter, and novelist living in Calais, Vermont. Two of his chapbooks have been published by Wood Thrush Books, and his poems have appeared most recently in *Mizna*, *The Shanghai Literary Review*, and *The World Engaged*.

All Too Often
Barbara S. Johnson

My arm ached after the 42-minute hold working my way up, then down to the bottom of the wait order, then up again. Finally, "Hello?"

"Oh thank goodness, a real person!" For the first time in weeks, my chest relaxed. "Let me explain. The refrigerator I purchased in November was delivered late December, broken. Still broken and it's mid-January. It seems to be leaking some four odor. We all have headaches."

"Ma'am?"

"We've tried calling the repair number multiple times, but no one followed up."

"Ma'am?"

"My complaints have been passed from person to person. I've kept a log; eleven calls, seven messages. I filed a report on the website and spent hours on the phone."

"Ma'am?"

"Please help get this thing removed and replaced. I don't think I can stand it one more day."

"Ma'am. You've reached the janitor. You'll have to call back Monday."

BARBARA S. JOHNSON
ALL TOO OFTEN

Barbara's works include professional articles (physical therapy), children's book (editor and illustrator), poems and stories in *Alaska Women Speak*, *The Binnacle* (2016) and *Alaska Writers Guild website*. She was the AWG Writer of the Year 2014, 2015, 2016 (tied). She wrote this story after a long struggle purchasing a treadmill.

MOMMA
KAYSSIE K.

I carried momma down the steps, taking longer than I usually do, even with the bike. She says she carried me in her belly for months, not whining like me. So I didn't complain, supporting your momma is like "having cupcakes handed to you" she says.

We stopped a minute when the air from outside slapped our faces. We always had to do that. I think it's because you get used to the smell of momma, the smell of her pills, a wetted bed and potatoes, and you sometimes forget what the actual world smells like.

She must've seen me lead her to the swing because sh-she said something like,

"No, let's sleep on the grass this time. I want to see the stars."

I remember we laid there for a while. When I felt a puddle form beneath my dress. I turned to momma and m-momma...

Momma was gone.

KAYSSIE K.
MOMMA

Kayssie K. is a young writer and marketing student with a passion for all things obscure and challenging. She has been published in numerous magazines such as the *Seventh Wave*, *NotSoPopular*, and *Womanhood*. She is also a founder of the Royal Integrity Collective which promotes self-love and self-awareness through art.

UNCERTAINTY
STANLEY KORN

A student of quantum mechanics
Could not comprehend its dynamics;
So uncertain was he
Of E and of p,
He gave up and studied ceramics.

STANLEY KORN
UNCERTAINTY

Stanley Korn received a B.S. in physics from the Rensselaer Polytechnic Institute. He was employed by DoD as an operations research analyst and was the coordinator of the Mensa Parapsychology SIG. He is the author of two books, an inventor with four issued patents, and a Fellow of the ISPE.

THE BUNKER
LAURIE MERRITT LARKIN

Reaching the bunker, Fawn dropped her bags of bitter apples and raised the bunker door. Jake and a wounded Rick stumbled down the dirt stairs first. Fawn retrieved the apples and descended, lowering the door.

She reached into a crevice in the wall for a candle. It was deathly quiet. She whispered to the hungry, waiting children to let them know it was the older three. She lit the candle stub, quelled the darkness and revealed the first few, tiny faces emerging into the circle of light. The faces were starved, terrified. They burst forward, straining toward their protectors, horror etched in their tiny, sunken features. Fawn bent down to wrap her arms around them. She had brought food.

From the gloom behind the faces of the terrified children, the smiters moved into the candle light. Each wielded an ugly weapon.

A few apples would not save them this time.

LAURIE MERRITT LARKIN
THE BUNKER

Laurie Merritt Larkin is a UMM alumnus living the dream in Topfield, Maine. She has always been interested in writing, especially short stories, ultra-shorts, and children's books. A recent move and change in circumstances, she is hoping, will allow her more time for writing.

TRAFFIC
DOUG MATHEWSON

I'm second car at the light, the first a police car. The officer fusses with his hair in the rearview. He fusses, he musses. Slick the sides back and repeat. Playfully he arranges his forelock, and then plucks it forward twice more. No, three times.

The light is green, should I blow the horn?

DOUG MATHEWSON
TRAFFIC

Doug Mathewson likes to stay home with his wife and their two cats and do as little real work as possible. His stories have appeared here and there, now and then, in publications around the world and perhaps beyond. More of his fiction can be found at www.little2say.org, *True Stories From Imaginary Lives*.

LAST HARVEST
CAROLINE MICHALICKI

Jeb and Lena owned the fifty acres and farmed the field for over sixty years. The last five years (due to Jeb's age and bad back) the land had gone fallow.

"Don't ya think it's time for us to leave this place?" Lena suggested.

"To do what?" Jeb grew angry.

He knew Lena wanted to move to an apartment close to town. She hated being dependent on her only neighbor to run her errands.

"I know what you're thinking." Jeb struggled out of his chair, hobbled to the barn and started the tractor.

Lena opened the screen door and yelled, "What are you doing, you stubborn, old goat?"

Jeb couldn't hear her over the roar of the engine. He drove into the high grass.

Lena fell asleep in her rocker on the porch waiting for Jeb to come home. The sun rose. Lena never woke. Jeb never returned.

CAROLINE MICHALICKI
LAST HARVEST

Caroline Michalicki resides in rural Georgia with her husband, their old lab, Rudy and Radar, a stray pup that found their pack.

INTERN
DOUGLAS W. MILLIKEN

It's something dreamlike and lovely, how the IV's hollow tip submerges so purposefully into the back of T's right hand. "Time was, I'd see a group of boys on the street, white boys, any boys, really, kids enjoying themselves real loud, taking up the whole sidewalk, I'd look at them coming and wonder, *Is this it, is this the time?*" T smiles at the nurse, teeth white and straight. "Never know, is it more foolish to be afraid or not be afraid?" Or anyway, what teeth are left. "Like, TV violence is still violence, you know? It being cliché don't make it any less real." But the nurse has already walked away, replaced by someone else. The dreamish needle setting all edges a-blur. "Never thought it'd ever actually be the time."

DOUGLAS W. MILLIKEN
INTERN

Douglas W. Milliken is the author of the novel *To Sleep as Animals* and several chapbooks, most recently *One Thousand Owls Behind Your Chest*. His stories have been honored by the Maine Literary Awards, the Pushcart Prize, and *Glimmer Train*, as well as published in dozens of journals, including *Slice*, the *Collagist*, and the *Believer*, among others. www.douglaswmilliken.com.

BROKEN VESSELS
ELLEN BIRKETT MORRIS

It is true we love
Because of imperfection
Not in spite of it

Your mother's hand wrapped around
The chipped milk glass mug
Her knuckles swollen with arthritis

The shirt stained with tomato
Bitter sauce your wife cooked
With care just for you

Bent pages of the book
Your notes in the margins
What are my dreams?

The worn spot in the kitchen floor
Where your parents danced
His chin resting on her head

Nothing is untouched by time or wear
Each smudge or crack reveals
A certain grace

ELLEN BIRKETT MORRIS
BROKEN VESSELS

Ellen Birkett Morris is the author of *Surrender (*Finishing Line Press). Her poetry is forthcoming in *Thin Air Magazine* and has appeared in *The Clackamas Literary Review*, *Juked*, *Alimentum*, *Gastronomica*, and *Inscape*. Morris won top prize in the 2008 Binnacle Ultra-Short Edition and was a semi-finalist for the 2009 Rita Dove Poetry Prize.

THE PAINTING
BEKI MUCHOW

Emma woke, taking in her surroundings. Yes. A hotel. She noticed the painting on the wall, recalling the strange affect it had on her as she sat staring at it the night before. No doubt it was the catalyst for her dream of a pleasant walk through a quiet village, a glass of wine at a sidewalk cafe, a long walk on a quiet beach, the warm water gently lapping around her ankles, soaking her pant legs. She stretched and tossed the covers back looking forward to the first day of her vacation, albeit far from any beaches. Throwing her feet over the side of the bed, she was surprised to find her pant legs rolled up and the shoes beside her bed full of sand.

BEKI MUCHOW
THE PAINTING

Beki Muchow lives and writes in Sherwood, Oregon. She is currently working on a novel and a collection of short stories.

CONDOLENCES 2
JAMES B. NICOLA

My heart goes to the family of the dead. (And to the dying.)
But how he took our breath away risking all by driving
without a safety belt. (Once, twice—well, once too often, surely,
the last time being his last race as you know—which he nearly
won, didn't he? What happened was, they'd changed the
        regulation,
but he did not adhere because it was not his tradition,
I guess, to fasten the safety belt. So he sped round and round,
and crashed. And oh the loss we felt when his body was found.

Some call him hero. I can't say that word, for had he fastened
his, he'd still be alive today. But who has ever listened
to common sense, or what's not said, certainly not Dale Senior,
so why his fans, now that he's dead? No, let us root for Junior,
a hero if sports ever had one. How the bleachers rise
to cheer him on and go half-mad and buy his merchandise.)

JAMES B. NICOLA
CONDOLENCES 2

James B. Nicola's poems have appeared in *The Binnacle*, *Antioch Review*, *Southwest Review*, *Atlanta Review*, *Rattle*, *Tar River*, and *Poetry East*. His nonfiction book *Playing the Audience* won a Choice award. His first full-length poetry collection is *Manhattan Plaza* (2014); his second, *Stage to Page: Poems from the Theater* (2016).

His four poetry collections are *Manhattan Plaza* (2014), *Stage to Page: Poems from the Theater* (2016), *Wind in the Cave* (2017), and *Out of Nothing: Poems of Art and Artists* (2018). Visit sites.google.com/site/jamesbnicola.

THE DROWNINGS
CHRISTOPHER OWEN

He'd gone out to sea three days back, he and his crew, fishing the Irish Sea from out of Liverpool, caught up in thick fog, their bodies found forty-six miles out. The deckhand's young wife Gwyneth inconsolable, lost in grief. It was dawn, barely after six, her head and arms across her mother's lap, the Bible open on the table, for her mother was a woman held to the comfort of the Lord Jesus Christ. Outside the front door, ~~having~~ knocked gently, the Methodist Minister, but the girl - she was eighteen - had no thought of him, of Jesus, but only of Thomas in the deep, with no children to fulfil their promise. There was knocking at the door but neither woman stirred.

CHRISTOPHER OWEN
THE DROWNINGS

Trained at RADA. Actor for 55 years. Published stories in anthology by Jessica Kingsley Publishers, *Neon Magazine*, *Smoke Magazine*, *Irish Literary Review*, *Valve Journal*. Plays: 2016: *Touch of A Butterfly's Wing* long-listed Papatango Award; *Still Waters* at Manhattan Theatre, New York. Others in Manchester, Australia, Ireland, etc. Website: www.christopherowen.co.uk

SALT LICK, FEBRUARY 26, 1940
ASHLEY PARKER OWENS

Fourteen forestry workers
witness a horseshoe-shaped rig
lift an elk out of the forest.

The horseshoe blots the haunting dark,
hiding constellations,
then withers—
against the backdrop of dawn,
dark silhouette versus first light.

Hiding in the succulent woods
the workers watch the horseshoe drift away
in elegant escape with the elk drooping,
unconscious.

Hesitant to reject the experience,
they return to work,
no discussion of their observation,
the uncaring sky now an empty enigma.

ASHLEY PARKER OWENS
SALT LICK, FEBRUARY 26, 1940

Ashley Parker Owens is a writer, poet, and UFO abductee living in Richmond, Kentucky.

SECONDHAND INSPIRATION
ADRIAN S. POTTER

The wild-haired woman and I touch fingers briefly. We are both reaching for the same novel, forest green cover with a slightly weathered spine. "Hey, I saw it first," I assert.

"It was my father's," she retorts. She emphatically shows me the initials scrawled on the first page, then awkwardly hefts a stack of hardbacks. "I'm trying to buy him back."

"You mean his books."

"Is there a difference? You're defined by what you read."

I retreat, thinking about the dollar in my wallet, about how I pretend to be well-read despite not owning a single classic. Outside the bookstore, I'm so glad her dad is dead that I smile. I don't want his life, not anymore.

ADRIAN S. POTTER
SECONDHAND INSPIRATION

Adrian S. Potter writes poetry and short fiction. He is the author of the fiction chapbook *Survival Notes* (Červená Barva Press, 2008) and winner of the 2010 Southern Illinois Writers Guild Poetry Contest. Some publication credits include *North American Review*, *Obsidian*, and *Kansas City Voices*. He blogs, sometimes, at http://adrianspotter.com/.

MISSED CALL
ANDREA REEVES

The car left the road. I heard the crash. Stunned, I pulled my car to the shoulder. The first on the scene. I threw open my door and ran to the figure that laid broken in the road. A young girl.

Rain came down in sheets, it beat down and ran down the back collar of my raincoat. My knees ground into the black asphalt. The scene illuminated by my headlights.

Her hand felt cold in mine. I squeezed it harder. Black metal twisted around the telephone pole, thrown from the wreckage. Sirens blared in the distance, their bubblegum lights appeared through the sideways rain.

Too late, I felt her life leave her young body. She took her last breath. Her iPhone blinked nearby.

Missed call.

ANDREA REEVES
MISSED CALL

Andrea Reeves received a Columbia Scholastic Gold Circle Award for her feature cover story on "Adoption" for the first edition of her high school magazine Images. Her short stories have won weekly challenges in the writing group she's a member of on Facebook. Her published fiction books *The Devil On Two Wheels*, *Chasing The Storm* and *One Bottle of Merlot* are available on Amazon. She enjoys both reading and writing fiction. She's a new author who resides in Texas with her husband, Mark.

A DREAM OF ROME
RACHEL RODMAN

It was the fashion in those times, recalling the grandeur of Rome and the non-conventional childhood of Romulus, its founder, for parents to entrust their own offspring to wolves.

As swaddling cloth, the parents used silken fabrics, monogrammed with the family crest. They wrapped, with particular care, the little hands, which would one day build iconic civilizations.

In hollows, by the river, the parents set their bundles. Before leaving, they waited for the telltale glitter of teeth, set in the underbrush—evidence of a she-wolf, waiting to complete the adoption.

"Be great," they instructed their babies, by way of goodbye.

Rachel Rodman
A Dream of Rome

Rachel Rodman's fiction has appeared in *The Future Fire*, *Daily Science Fiction*, *Grievous Angel*, and elsewhere. Read more at www.rachelrodman.com.

HER TRAIN DERAILED
SHANNON SCHUREN

Her train derailed just after she'd gotten the call from Finn. He was sorry. That other woman had been a mistake, a temporary insanity. Pre-wedding jitters.

Staring at the wreckage as it smoked and smoldered, Sloane caught a glimpse of an old woman in the glass of one of the windows that hadn't shattered. She touched herself as if she'd lost her sight and watched the stranger do the same. Brittle hair. Chapped lips. Cheeks, breasts, stomach, elbows.

They'll be sending another train along, the attendant said. We can board and be on our way. Put this unpleasantness behind us, he said.

Get right back on and keep hurtling into the future. The memory of the crash would fade with each retelling. Soon she'd have only the distorted reflection of herself growing older in the midst of the wreckage.

Sloane waited until his back was turned before she started walking.

SHANNON SCHUREN
HER TRAIN DERAILED

Shannon Schuren is a librarian in Sheboygan Falls, Wisconsin. Her short stories have appeared in previous Ultra-Short editions, as well as other literary journals. She also writes longer fiction. Her debut novel, *The Virtue of Sin*, is forthcoming from Philomel/Penguin Random House in 2019.

GHOSTWRITER
SAGE

I hadn't planned to spend Easter brunch in a basement with my hands cuffed to an Underwood Touchmaster Five with a "J" key that stuck, but there I was, surrounded by others in a dimly lit cellar, the smell of Anna's oil still on me. I can't say how long I've been here, but I can say we—the other ghostwriters and myself—spend every day waiting for James Patterson to come with water and news of the outside world. His true form is hideous. We're forbidden to talk about Patterson's sixteen heads, or the million arms he lashes us with. If our story is successful, we are rewarded with sunlight. I hear the Alex Cross people upstairs even have bread. I've been compiling this record on toilet paper during my once daily restroom break. People need to know. I hear his hoofed third leg on the stairs. Send help.

SAGE
GHOSTWRITER

Sage is an MFA candidate and Teaching Fellow at St. Mary's College in California. Their work appears in *North American Review*, *Penn Review*, *Pittsburgh Poetry Review*, *The Rumpus*, and elsewhere.

THE DENOUEMENT OF MR. POTATO HEAD
MAUREEN SHERBONDY

Mr. Potato Head falls off the desk. It is all too much – streams of paperwork, computer glitches, that dizzying spinning throbber icon that throws him off balance. What choice does he have? Hide beneath clutter? Return to the box? He longs for halcyon factory days, born from the metal mold of his mother; he wants to melt into that embryonic plastic state when the machinery of life was only a distant hum.

MAUREEN SHERBONDY
THE DENOUEMENT OF MR. POTATO HEAD

Maureen Sherbondy teaches English at a community college in North Carolina. Her most recent book is *Belongings*.

THE SILLINESS OF LOVE
DIANE SMITH

Moments move swiftly
Frolicking in clover
Such wild, sweet kisses
Crashing all around

Quakes ripple skin to the edge
Soft tendrils of hair
Curl in fingers
and thoughts

Tickles, light shrill laughter
Honeysuckle branches
Brushing, tapping with the breeze
Ah, the silliness of love

DIANE SMITH
THE SILLINESS OF LOVE

Diane Smith is the principal editor and founder of Grey Sparrow Press. She writes about the homeless, immigration, the poor, the diminishing middle class, healthcare; those who have little visibility or power in society. Smith graduated from Harvard University (2017) with a Master of Liberal Arts in the field of Journalism.

BEAUTICEUTICALS
JENNA PASHLEY SMITH

From: research@beauticeuticalstherapeutic.com
To: <girlfriend1>
Subject: Product List

Becca,

Lucky girl! You made clinical trials. Pick your poison below.

-Megawatt lipgloss: doubles as toothpaste to eliminate plaque and brighten enamel with genetically engineered piranha DNA. May help prevent some lip cancers.

-Powdered Pill bronzer: 74.3% effective in preventing unwanted pregnancies.

-Precise Pallor concealer: blood pressure regulator.

-Feverish blush: patented antiviral medication for instant superflu relief.

-InsuLash mascara: time-release insulin and mink fiber dyes for long-wearing coverage.

-Color Me Thin nail polish, five shades: suppresses appetite for up to seven days.

-Mood powder: prescription-free multitasking. Gold-flecked Summer Daze combines sunscreen with a mild stimulant; silver Fairy Dust is infused with anti-wrinkle technology and muscle relaxers.

Testing starts next week; I'll make sure you're in the treatment group. Can't wait to see the change in you!

Love,
Stan

p.s. Waiver attached. Boring fine print stuff, just sign on the x and return. You'll be fine.

JENNA PASHLEY SMITH
BEAUTICEUTICALS

Jenna Pashley Smith's award-winning poems have appeared in diverse publications, including *The Binnacle*, *Eastern Iowa Review*, *Encore*, *Texas Poetry Calendar*, and others. She lives in Houston, Texas where she is a member of the SCBWI, the Poetry Society of Texas, and a weekly critique group.

CHANGE
MATTHEW J. SPIRENG

It's 8 a.m. on a weekday slightly off-season
in Provincetown and the attendant at the all-day
parking lot where you pay five dollars in advance
for the first two hours and the rest when you leave

doesn't have change for a twenty. We're
the first car of the day and he doesn't have change
for a twenty. If we hadn't parked here before
and I didn't know he was the regular attendant

I might think he was someone who snuck
into the booth before the regular attendant got here
and was grabbing a little cash for his breakfast.
How can you start the day in a business

in a busy tourist town—even slightly off-season—
with no change for a twenty-dollar bill?
We dig around in my wallet and her purse
and come up with five dollars. Now he can break a ten.

MATTHEW J. SPIRENG
CHANGE

Matthew J. Spireng's books are *What Focus Is* from Word Tech Communications and *Out of Body*, winner of the 2004 Bluestem Poetry Award, and the chapbooks *Clear Cut*, *Young Farmer*, *Encounters*, *Inspiration Point*, and *Just This*. He is an eight-time Pushcart Prize nominee.

WHAT CAN I SAY?
ERIK SVEHAUG

I didn't take anything. I'm waiting for a friend of mine.

Yeah, I have a wrench under my coat.

No, I don't have a receipt for it. It just looks like one of yours.

So you're stuck with me. How long does this usually take?

Look, I just blew it. Just kick me out. It's cool.

I'm sick of waiting; where's the "man" when you want him?

Changing of the guard, eh?

They've had me in here for over an hour.

I'm so sorry. Can't I just pay for it and never come into the store again?

Sorry about the tears, man. My kid is so hungry and what if I lose my place? We'd be on the street!

But you can do something, can't you? I won't ever come in here again, I swear!

Thank you so much, man! I won't ever do anything this stupid again. Really!

ERIK SVEHAUG
WHAT CAN I SAY?

Erik Svehaug, a Santa Cruzan, writes poetry and short fiction. He is moved by Indigenous rights and unheralded individuals. Compassion, audacity, and curiosity inspire him and he loves word music. His published work is collected at www.eriksvehaug.com. This is his fifth Ultra-Short appearance.

THE OLD HOUSE
R.M. TRENKLER-THOMSON

The broker greeted the couple at the entrance of a gorgeous, old house, at the end of the street, bordered by a forest and creek. DeShawn gazed at his finance, a look she knew well. "Let's see the inside first," Emma cautioned.

The living room was small but had a fireplace into which, suddenly, something fell with a thud. Startled, they proceeded to the kitchen where they found the refrigerator open, food scraps everywhere. The broker apologized, assuring this wasn't how it looked yesterday, when they heard a loud hoot upstairs. They all left, fast.

The raccoon emerged from behind the fridge, the mouse from the fireplace, sooty. The owl flew down the staircase and asked, "Should we have been quieter?" "No," replied the raccoon. "Looks like they just finished college. No kids, no pets, probably a party every day. We won't get a wink of sleep."

R.M. TRENKLER-THOMSON
THE OLD HOUSE

R.M. Trenkler-Thomson emigrated from Germany to the United States in the 1990's. After a long career in information technology, in 2015 he began attending workshops and writer groups at libraries and a local writers center. He is preparing to publish a collection of stories and poems with his writing colleagues.

SHARON AT HER WORST
CAROLINE TODD

Sharon did not recall the photograph, much less understand why it was in her parents' photo album. Sharon would have left the album on the shelf had she known that this picture of her, passed out drunk next to a full ashtray, would accompany family portraits and pictures from dance recitals.

Sharon's daughter asked, "Who's that guy lying next to you?"

"It's a friend"— a friend whom she had dated during the last summer she had spent at home. It was the summer of 1987, a season of unprotected sex, heavy smoking, and underage drinking.

Sharon's mother had captioned the photo, *Sharon at her worst.* Sharon smirked at her mother's preservation of such a moment; her mother always acknowledged the bad with the good. However, there was no *Sharon at her best* caption; there were just smiling faces and permed hair.

CAROLINE TODD
SHARON AT HER WORST

Caroline Todd and her husband live in Kingston, Ontario, Canada, with their two young children. Caroline has had short stories appear in *Shoreline*, *The Binnacle* and *Canadian Tales of the Fantastic* (Volume IV).

WAR OF THE ROSES
DONNA TURELLO

Old McGillicuddy's roses are legendary, if only for the ivy. But comes the day this young buck buys the place next door. The missus has big plans. A greenhouse window over the sink, facing McGillicuddy's.

The landscaper rips out McGillicuddy's roses. But the ivy won't go. It's all entangled around the rusted fence. Which belongs to McGillicuddy.

What a sound, the iron posts crashing. Caterpillar ripped up fence and all, along with half of McGillicuddy's driveway.

Well, there was quite a falling out. Yelling, much waving of hammers as the missus stood grinning in her kitchen window.

Everybody thought that the end. Until McGillicuddy planted new rosebushes. *Lucky seven,* he always said. Of course, where there'd been seven, now stand seven *hundred.*

Next spring, the ivy returned with a vengeance, climbing the stalks of the roses, which stood in place of the fence.

The young folk hadn't dug deep enough.

DONNA TURELLO
WAR OF THE ROSES

Donna L. Turello holds an M.A. in English Lit and is working on several novels and scripts. She's been published in *Best Short Stories from the Saturday Evening Post 2015; Wow! Women on Writing; Chicken Soup for the Soul: My Resolution; Patchwork Path: Treasure Box;* and *Patchwork Path: Christmas Stocking.*

SHE MARCHED
ReLYNN VAUGHN

Her feet cracked like thunder on the cobbled streets of Paris. Each step rang out in time with her sisters. No more would her children starve. No more would she hear their cries.

She marched.

Her boots trod the streets in Washington, her white dress dancing around her feet. Even as they drug her sisters away, imprisoned them, forced tubes down their throats. Let them take her today.

She marched.

Her patented leather shoes pinched her toes down the Alabama highway. Past the police with dogs. Past men screaming for her blood. In the footsteps of Dr. King, for her rights, and for her children. Even in the wake of poor Pastor Reeb's death.

She marched.

Her feet made little sound in her sneakers. On the streets of New York and Los Angeles, Louisville and Denver, London and Tokyo. For her health. For education. For peace for all.

She marched.

ReLynn Vaughn
She Marched

ReLynn was born in Northern California and grew up where the South meets the American West. She now lives near Puget Sound.

End Notes

The Ultra-Short Competition, *The Binnacle*, and, strictly speaking, the University of Maine at Machias have come to an end. The journal was a free-standing periodical for nearly fifty years and existed in earlier forms for eleven more. So it goes.

Though this is the last edition of *The Binnacle*, the Ultra-Short will continue as a publication of the Primavera Press.

I wish to thank all of those who have contributed to the competition and the nearly fifty volumes I have edited for the press over eighteen years. You have been an inspiration to me and a true gift to all who have had the good fortune to read your words.

My Best to All,

Gerard P. NeCastro
Binnacle Editor